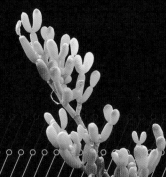

• Start TO Finish
Second Series

FROM Seed TO Cactus

● LISA OWINGS

LERNER PUBLICATIONS ▸ Minneapolis

TABLE OF Contents

Lerner Publications Company
A division of Lerner Publishing Group, Inc.
241 First Avenue North
Minneapolis, MN 55401 USA

For reading levels and more information, look up this title at www.lernerbooks.com.

Library of Congress Cataloging-in-Publication Data

Names: Owings, Lisa, author.
Title: From seed to cactus / Lisa Owings.
Other titles: Start to finish (Minneapolis, Minn.). Second series.
Description: Minneapolis, MN : Lerner Publications Company, [2017] | Series: Start to finish. Second series | Includes bibliographical references and index.
Identifiers: LCCN 2016038899 (print) | LCCN 2016041148 (ebook) | ISBN 9781512434453 (lb : alk. paper) | ISBN 9781512450972 (eb pdf)
Subjects: LCSH: Cactus—Life cycles—Juvenile literature.
Classification: LCC QK495.C11 O94 2017 (print) | LCC QK495.C11 (ebook) | DDC 583/.56—dc23

LC record available at https://lccn.loc.gov/2016038899

Manufactured in the United States of America
1-42094-25388-10/20/2016

A Cactus is a desert plant.   How does it grow?

First, a cactus seed sprouts.

Animals spread the seeds of a cactus across a desert. Only a few land where conditions are right for growing. After weeks or months, a new cactus **shoot** curls out of a seed.

Then a tiny seedling appears.

A seedling is a young cactus plant. A set of puffy leaves pushes through the soil. Soon a small, fuzzy ball appears between them. The cactus plant is just starting to form.

Roots grow in the ground.

The roots spread widely and keep close to the surface. After a rain, the roots bring water and **nutrients** to the growing cactus.

The cactus grows larger.

In the first months, the cactus starts looking more like the prickly plants you may have seen. Its first set of leaves disappears beneath a stem bristling with **spines**. But the plant is still very small.

The cactus takes on a shape.

As the cactus gets bigger, it takes on the shape it will have once it is fully grown. A cactus can be rounded. It can have branching parts that look like arms. No two **cacti** look exactly alike.

In spring, the cactus flowers bloom.

Large cactus flowers bring bursts of color to the desert. The flowers often stay open for only a day. Insects, birds, and bats **pollinate** the flowers.

Soon the cactus fruit ripens.

Pollinated flowers drop from the cactus. Colorful fruits with seeds inside grow in their place. Birds and other animals eat the fruit and scatter the seeds across the desert.

The cactus keeps growing for many years.

The cactus keeps growing little by little. Some cacti grow branches. Others produce clusters of plants. Some grow extremely tall.

Finally, it is fully grown!

Some cacti can live for more than one hundred years. They provide food and shelter for desert animals. People enjoy their unusual beauty. A great way to learn more about cacti is to grow your own!

Glossary

cacti: the word for more than one cactus plant. *Cactus* is the word for one cactus plant.

nutrients: substances that plants, animals, and people need to live and grow

pollinate: to place pollen on a plant so it can form seeds

ripens: becomes fully grown and developed

seedling: a young plant

shoot: a part of a new plant that is just starting to grow

spines: sharp, pointy parts on plants or animals

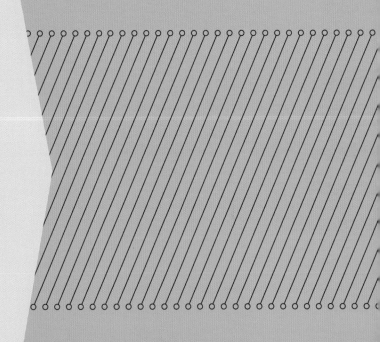

22

Further Information

Anza-Borrego: Desert Plants
http://www.abdnha.org/just-for-kids/anza-borrego-just-for-kids-plants.htm
Check out this site to learn more about desert plants.

CactiGuide.com
http://cactiguide.com/habitsearch
Did you find or grow a cactus but aren't sure what kind it is? Use this site
to find out!

Gray, Rita. *Flowers Are Calling*. Boston: Houghton Mifflin Harcourt, 2015.
Beautiful illustrations show how cactus blooms and other flowers are
pollinated.

PBS Kids: Cactus
http://pbskids.org/dragonflytv/show/cactus.html
Follow Mark and Alex to the Arizona-Sonora Desert Museum to learn
about the saguaro cactus and other things that live in the desert.

Silverman, Buffy. *Let's Visit the Desert*. Minneapolis: Lerner Publications,
2017. Learn about the world's deserts and desert wildlife in this book.

Index

Photo Acknowledgments

The images in this book are used with the permission of: © F1 online digitale Bildagentur/Alamy, p. 1; © arka38/Shutterstock.com, p. 3; © Guilermo Lopez Barrera/Alamy, p. 5; © iStockphoto.com/Bernd Schmidt, p. 7; © Grant Heilman Photography/Alamy, p. 9; © iStockphoto.com/winbio, p. 11; © Craig Lovell/Eagle Visions Photography/Alamy, p. 13; © fstockfoto/Shutterstock.com, p. 15; © piXXart/Shutterstock.com, p. 17; © StillsByScott/Shutterstock.com, p. 19; © Elena Rostunova/Shutterstock.com, p. 21;

Front cover: © iStockphoto.com/rtrible.

Main body text set in Arta Std Book 20/26.
Typeface provided by International Typeface Corp.

LERNER
e
SOURCE™

Expand learning beyond the printed book. Download free, complementary educational resources for this book from our website, www.lerneresource.com.